TAILS OF THE TERRIER

Poems of Terrier Appreciation

Alexia Muelle-Rushbrook

2020

Printed by
Leiston Press Ltd
Masterlord Ind. Est.
Leiston
Suffolk
IP16 4JD
www.leistonpress.com

ISBN: 978-1-911311-69-0

Written and first published in the UK 2020

Written by Alexia Muelle-Rushbrook

Photographs by Alexia Muelle-Rushbrook

I dedicate this book to every dog that has ever blessed me by walking with me through my life. Their love, joy and laughter has touched my soul in a way that cannot be fully described. Particular dedication must go to Stan, who started my passion of all things terrier and to Queenie, who took terrier appreciation to a whole new level. I cannot forget my husband, Sergio, who introduced terriers to me in the first place and without his love and support, this book would never be.

I hope anyone who reads this looking for a dog, finds the truth, humour and love that comes with life with a terrier.

Anyone with a terrier, I think you'll understand, and I hope it makes you laugh.

Long live the Terrier!

1. INTRODUCTION

Disclaimer

To Labrador and Spaniel
I apologise from the start
For if in this book I mock you
Know it's with no meanness in my heart
I really do appreciate
All your different ways
But this book is for the terrier
And all my merits praise!

Yes, you retrieve with gladness
The like of which I cannot tell
And are loyalty unspoken
You serve your guardians well
But where is the fun in life
If it isn't also spent with me?
The cheekiest of terrier
The best breed you'll ever see!

Thinking of a Puppy

So, you're thinking of a puppy
And researching before you buy?
That is definitely advisable
Let me tell you why...

As you read through your manual
Of each breeds' unique ways
If you pause on a terrier
You'll definitely need to heed what I say

The terrier maybe small and cute
The look that you adore
But are you really properly versed
On what can be in store?

Size may be an advantage
But big spirit - That may not?!
For we are not to be trifled with
Or simply trotted round the block

Our brains are ever ticking
Trouble we may find
Though when we have found it
It wasn't necessarily what we had in mind!

I hope you plan to train us
With consistency?
Because we will ever test your
Recalling ability!

Please don't get me wrong
We really are the best
But undoubtedly some days
We'll put your patience to the test!

If, however you smile
When you read this song
Then with a breed of terrier
You definitely cannot go wrong

So, please continue on your current journey
A journey of discovery
Of how fun life with a terrier
Can absolutely be!

T - is for Terrible - Oh, that can't be fair!
You mean Terrific or Tenacious or even Teddy bear?!
How can you mean Terrible? That is just unjust!
True, only 'Terrible' if you don't appreciate them - *which is a must!*
Appreciate their unique, charming, cheeky ways
And then Tremendous better describes all their days

E - is for Earnest, for I know very well
They do not stop until a job is done and their energy is quelled
Ever ready, is also apt, I must say
As they are always ready for joy each day

R - is for Roar, for they have lots to say
On occasion, too much but at the end of the day
They were bred to alert so, to moan is hardly fair
And mostly they are just chatty - and enjoy to share!

R - is for Ridiculously cute – ha, I forced that one! - But what can I do?
Terriers are gorgeous, regardless of breed - it is true!
Such cheeky charmers, you can't ignore
When they are present, them will you adore!

I - is for Independent – of that there is no doubt!
Loyal and loving but that doesn't mean immediate recall when you shout!
Busy little people, with minds of their own
Intelligent and thoughtful, with a spirit that can't be outgrown

E - is for Entertaining – Comedians are they!
Rarely a dull moment seeps into their day!
Even when dreaming, I'm sure they cook up
Mischief to cause once they have woken up!

R - is for Radiant – For character radiates from within
Shines in a way that cheers the soul, that is fortunate enough to be let in
Such loving, affectionate, characters are they
Where else to find the like? – I cannot say!

To be a Terrier

Apparently, I am a terrier
I'm not sure what that means?
I think it means I get a free pass
To do exactly what I please

So, I'm glad I am a terrier!
Because frankly, I must say
I had absolutely no intention
Of doing anything you say!

Appreciation

What does it mean to be a terrier?
I'm really not quite sure
I think we get a bad rep
From those who don't adore
A little bit of extra spark
A little fire from me
But all I want at the end of the day
Is a cuddle and belly rub or three!

What Are Terriers?

Rough and tumble
Pull and tug 'em
Hardy as can be
Strong and tough
Made of good stuff
That's what terriers be!
Ever ready
Fast and steady
Defiant? Yes, maybe!
Full of heart
From the very start
Handsome as can be!

The Terrier Alphabet

A – is for Active – there's not much else to say!

B – is for Busy – kinda goes with A!

C – is for Courageous - always ready to save

D – is for Digging – what they naturally love to do

E – is for Ever ready - always prepared for fun

F – is for Forgive – any misdemeanours that might be done!

G – is for Gorgeous – of course!

H – is for Hunt – what they were originally bred to do

I – is for Intelligent – that should never be in doubt

J – is for Joker – life is best when things are fun

K – is for King – ruling no matter what their size

L – is for Loyal – they're forever true

M - is for Merry - always happy little souls

N – is for Nutty – the best ones all are

O – is for Opinionated – they know their own mind

P – is for Perfect – or so they think!

Q – is for Quirky – always charming

R – is for Rough and tumble – Robust little dogs

S – is for Spirit – They have it in abundance!

T – is for Terrier – see the rest of A to Z!

U – is for Unique – no one else can compare

V- is for Valiant – always determined

X – is for Xcuse me – you'll probably say that at least once a day!

W- is for Wilful? -Possibly, but more misunderstood than anything, you know

Y - is for yap - for they can enjoy a chat

Z – is for Zippy – rarely are they slow

2. CONVERSATIONS WITH YOUR TERRIER

Latin

Terrier is Latin
For 'of the earth'
So tell me why you moan
When earth I like to turf?
It is literally in my title
I am not hiding a thing
I am stating from the beginning
My intentions do out ring!

I was Bred to Dig Things

I was bred to dig things
To hunt along your hedge
To seek out little critters
That you and I wished dead

I'm particularly good at dispatching
Little rats and mice
But am also good with others
They will not get to blink thrice!

I also hate pigeons
And critters that dare to pass
Across my sacred boundaries
And didn't stop to ask

Those horrid flappy birds
Sit stupidly up high
Daring to taunt me
Oh, if only they come down, I show them why!

I am the King of all I see
Be not fooled by my small size
I am a terrier!
To cross me, is generally unwise!

I maybe small and sparky
Not all may understand
My level of intelligence
And value me for all I am

But I am a Terrier!
In charge of all I see
Ever loyal and loving
Happy and carefree!

Communication

I understand your moves
Do you understand mine?
I see all of yours
I watch all the time
With you communicating
If only you'd see
I am talking
As clear as can be!

I know

I understand just what you say
Be in no doubt of that, ok?
For even when you spell it out
I understand what you're about!

I also read your body signs
For how you move, is just a mime
I can read you like a book
I understand your every look

So, please do not make the mistake
Of thinking I don't undertake
All your words and little ways
Through them you are clear as day!

I know exactly what you're about
Be it whisper, be it shout
Whether it be walk, food, work or play
I know exactly what you say!

The Importance of Play

The importance of play
I can't understate
The importance of happy brain
You cannot overrate

Do not over exercise me
When I'm still small
Give my bones time to mature
And grow good joints and all

Instead play with me
Exercise my brain
Train and stimulate me
Teach me all kinds of games

So many great places
Of which we'll have to tell
You can just look, while treasures
I run around and smell

Just remember not to over exercise me
There is plenty of time, you will see
Plenty of time, to build me up
To a strong adult, from a very cute puppy!

My Nose Is Made For Sniffing

My nose was made for sniffing
And sniffing it must do
If I don't get to sniff things
My nose has nothing to do

My brain likes me to sniff things
It keeps me happy and bright
Even if I sniff things
That you might not quite like

My nose was made to sniff things
All creatures great and small
From the smallest of scents
To the biggest of them all

My nose was made to sniff things
Just so I can enjoy
The aromas all around me
And find my favourite toy!

My nose was made to sniff things
When we're out and about
So please don't pull and rush me
There's things I must sniff out!

So why not have a game with me?
So we might both enjoy
My ability to sniff things
Especially my favourite toy!

Come Rain or Shine

Come rain or shine
Your time is mine
To playtime be true
I'm ready for you!

Maybe not
If it's too hot
We can just wait
To go out the gate

Early play
Is better that day
Or really late
When the sun is sedate

It's raining hard
You can't mean charge?
I'll stay inside
Request denied!

No, I don't need to pee
You can't force me!
Fine, then get your coat!
We might need a big boat

Ah, it's not so bad
A good time can be had!
Oh, you're not having fun?
What a shame, what can be done?

It turns out, I'm in my prime
So, I will take my sweet time
Go in? No, not yet
Not until, we're both quite wet!

Now inside, I will shake
So, you make no mistake
Next time, inside we can stay
Until it is a fine day!

Come rain or shine
You are still mine!
So, let's start the day
Come on, let's play!

The Sleeping Terrier

We look like sleeping mountains
In a hazy daze
Not ready for anything
Certainly not for play

Do not be fooled by appearances
We hear your every move
We know what you are doing
What are you trying to prove?

Open a single packet
Or dare to try and leave
We'll be there right beside you
For every crumb of cheese

You'll realise we are ready
Always prepared to please
Armed to defend you
Against a band of thieves

People may try to dismiss us
Just because we are small
Ha! Little do they realise
We are for One and All!

Morning Has Broken

Morning has broken
Is that a song?
The blackbird has spoken
It's time to move on
For while we have slumbered
There's lots that have been free
Many leaving a calling card
A sign, out for me
All insubordinate
Creatures I hate
But they amuse me
So that makes us mates
Now that it's morning
And all is now bright
I do wish you'd get up
Even if you're a sight
Morning has broken
I'm sure that's a song?
Even if it is
It's time we move on
For the world
Well, it's calling
Is calling, you'll see
And we have much to find out
So, let's get to it!
You and me!

Bones

My teeth are oh, so shiny
Look at how they shine!
Yes, they are all natural
I clean them all the time!
I chew on a beef bone
The biggest I can find
It makes me oh, so happy
Please keep me well supplied!

Kibble

What is this thing you call kibble?
It hardly seems fair to me
For what is on your plate
Smells far better, indeed
I was taught that sharing
Was the way to go
In fact, I can only be caring
If I help spread the load

You really are quite selfish
That is quite a shock
For I was just preparing
For joys I thought in stock
It seems I am mistaken
There are no scraps for me
You really are so selfish
Not sharing your big tea!

Your waistline is expanding
To where I cannot tell
It just keeps on growing
If you eat like that, well?
It's hardly very surprising
But I have the remedy
You better start sharing
Some of your food with me!

Pocket Power

I smell it in your pocket
Oh, it smells so good!
If only you would feed me
You'd save me, yes you would!

Can't you see I'm wasting
No, Withering away?
If you don't hurry up
I will quite fade today!

If only you would give me
A treat, nay, say three!
Then you really would be
The saviour of me!

I smell it in your pocket
'Tis no good to anyone there!
Please just hand it over
For it is time to share!

Bathing

You may think I need bathing
But we don't quite agree
I'm pretty sure I am perfect
Just the way you see

You may think that I am scruffy
But that's ok by me
I don't need to be spotless
To dig and hunt and pee

Ok, I may be a little smelly
But I worked very hard on that
I rolled for a good half hour
In what came out of the neighbour's cat

Or was it that fat pigeon?
Or owl or duck or fox?
I particularly like the latter
Though his smell does linger round the blocks

I think that's why I like it?
But I must agree
That after a short while,
It can even bother me

That doesn't mean I want you
To come and shower me
I told you I've been working
On this odour - all for free!

Ok, I may be getting matted
You may just have a point
But please don't go and conclude
You haven't put my nose quite out of joint!

The Gardener

You can't be angry
I am just too cute
Cute and innocent
That is absolute!

Yes, I have been digging
In your flower bed
And by the greenhouse
Washing line and the shed

There were too many critters
Lying beneath, you see
So I dug them all up
Now they don't bother me

I've also made a wonderful
Basking hole, come see!
In it, I can soak up the sun
Whilst watching all about me

Don't worry about the garden
I don't mean to upstage
But a little terrier-forming
Is all the rage!

Bedtime

If you really meant it
I cannot really say
I know at the beginning
The rule to you, was clear as day

Clear you at least meant it
But clear as mud to me
For I never took it serious
I knew forever, it could not be

Once I could reach it
Jump or climb up on my own
You would see the error
Of trying to sleep alone

For now, by myself I reach it
And together we can sleep
You see the great advantage
Of sharing a place, your head to keep

My floor bed you see, it
Might be rather nice
But you don't seem to want to share it
So, at night I won't think twice

I know just where our comfort
Is best for all enjoyed
I think I might even bring
One of my favourite toys

Where Have You Been?

Ah, you have returned
Where have you been?
You cannot lie to me
I can smell all you've seen!

I know if you've been working
That is just fine
For there you earn our crust
A necessary use of time

But if you have been visiting
Friends without me
Then I am not amused
That is just treachery!

Yes, I will guard the home
When you are away
But take me for granted
You'll have the devil to pay!

Boom

I'm glad you are home
You'll never guess
What has happened
I am in such a stress!

I was woken
In such a start
What had happened?
I will impart!

As I bravely slept
In the living room
You'll never guess
My bed went BOOM!

Of my surprise
I cannot tell
For the fright
Knocked me over well

Now please don't look
At me like that
I feared you'd think
I'd had a spat!

The corner was
Already torn
When you bought it
I could have sworn

It was but cheaply made
And by a terrierist
It would seem, a trap was laid
A fearful one, for reason I don't know

To get me in trouble, I suppose?!
So, before you go into that room
Remember I love you
And it really did, just go BOOM!

Go Fetch

There are many ways
To truly enjoy my ball
I can amuse myself with it
But together brings joy for all

Fetch is the most common
A simple to and throw
But if you change it up
More amusement we will know

Hide and seek is always good
It helps me use my brain
Which you'll see is also good
As it keeps me from going insane

But one of my favourite games
You don't always seem to get
Is when I watch you find my ball
And you're the one to go fetch!

You think I should fetch it
At me you stand and stare
Hoping I will go run
All the way over there!

Ah, but no! You didn't realise
I was done for today
So, you can in actual fact
Go fetch yourself, ok?

Then, it is even better
If you didn't quite see
Where my ball landed
And you *really* do need me!

For I know exactly
Where that ball did land
But the burning question is
Will I go lend a hand?

A Confession

I hate to say I'm sorry
And admit a fault
But this one can't go unconfessed
So, sit down, with you I must consult

I saw upon the table
A lump I thought for me
I thought it was just oversight
It wasn't in my bowl already

So, I took it upon myself
To climb upon the chair
You see, that had been left out
With such apparent care!

The smell from below was inviting
But now it really thrilled, you see
So, there was no denying
That lump was meant for me!

To say it was delicious
Is to understate
The kind that's so nutritious
It didn't need to touch my plate!

Now, here comes the crunch
Why I see the error in my ways
It only now occurred to me
That is usually for Sundays

You see, I got the day wrong
I thought it too early
For the standard family roast
So, it must be my birthdee!

Now of course, I'm in my senses
I know that can't be yet
And it is in fact the weekend
How could I forget?

So, if I'm in error
Please don't start to shout
I did my best to clean up
And put it all in my mouth!

A Restless Night

Ah ha, at last, you are up!
It's been a busy night; I've been such a brave pup!
How so? I'm glad you asked!
There is a reason for that broken vase

For while you dreamt, I was on guard
And saved us all, as dangers did bombard
I checked the bin as it didn't smell right
I emptied it and searched half the night

Then my toy seemed to whine
So, I gutted it to see if it was fine
I ripped the squeaker out of its head
And now that toy is quite dead!

Then my bed whispered to me
Of evil thoughts that could not be
So, I told it who was boss
That's gone now, I don't feel the loss!

As apparently the sofa, will do just fine
I sleep there anyway most of the time!
I heard a hedgehog outside the door
What he wanted? - I am not sure!

I also thought I saw a cat
But come to think of it, it could have been a bat?
It doesn't matter, I told him all the same
He is not welcome and here, I reign!

Then the milkman came, and I watched him well
Just in case, at him I needed to yell
Lastly, I'm sorry I just couldn't help
But leave a poop - you didn't heed my yelp!

You fed me far too late last night
I was too full to hold on, all right?!
I am so sorry; I think it could be a bug
I'll just rest now, right on the rug

It'll need washing for I had trouble there too
I couldn't help it or wake up you!
But I saved us from many who would
Steal upon us and get up to no good

You are welcome, I'll save us any which way
Ever ready for work, rest and play
Just give me a minute and I will be
Ready for whatever the day holds, you'll see!

You'll Never Pee Alone

I think that it's time we had a chat
About when you go pee
And shut the door -Why is that?
It hardly seems fair, you see

For when I go, you stop and stare
Forever watching over me
Repeatedly repeating
Go wee, Go wee, Go wee!

Yes, I might need it
But my flow doesn't always come
Quite so easily when
I'm on the lookout for some fun

So, please hold on one sec
And have some patience please
For there're things that I need to check
Before it can flow free

Now, will you please explain it
Quietly to me?
Why I cannot follow you
When *you* need to go pee?

How can I protect you?
Or check around the floor?
If you keep on insisting
On shutting that darn door?

And please just reassure me
There's no secret hidden way
That you can leave unexpected
And in that room you'll stay?

I'll be out here patiently waiting
On guard until you're through
So, we're always close together
Close enough for both me and you

The Cleaner

You come out of the shower
Smelling oh, so sweet
But I think you missed a spot
So, I'll just lick your feet

I will do a better job
Than any scrubbing brush
Sit down and I'll show you
I'm not in any rush

Feet, face or neckline
I will gladly wash for you
And show my affection
A love that is so true

Hold Your Hand

I didn't bite
I just held your hand
I wish you would
Just understand

There are important
Things about
Things like me
There should be no doubt

Then you wouldn't
Get into a muddle
And you would just
Give me a cuddle

So, next time
Just understand
I was just trying
To hold your hand!

The Toy

Play don't eat
But how will I defeat
That squeaker that lies within?
Play, not crunch
But I like to munch
Don't tell me it's a sin!

Play not chew
But that really won't do
I'm sure you must've agreed
To only play and shake
Would be a mistake!?!
As chewing it really does need!

Possession

Hey, that's my shoe!

What is this?
No, that's not true!
You left it on the floor

If you leave it there
Tis only fair
It's mine to explore

I claim it's true
I'm sorry for you
But that is just the law!

Possession is mine
So, it's my time
To chew and chew, some more!

The Mistake

I've over done it this time
I should have shared my ball
But everyone was teasing
I didn't want to share at all

I took my ball away
And I did start to chew
I thought I'd just tease
But I chewed it quite through!

And now oh, the sorrow!
I really cannot tell
For that ball is quite stuck
And I don't feel well!

I enjoy chewing
It feels good in my mouth
But now, not so much
As it doesn't want to travel south!

If I have felt worse
I really don't know when!
Please take me to the vet
Oh, when *will* I be home again?

I have learnt my lesson
Chew all things small!
You say don't chew and swallow?
Ok, now where is my new ball?

The Tin

I am not dim
To my chagrin
I know what is in
The *yellow* tin!

No, not the blue
What have they done to you?
That is not wise
Teasing I do despise!

So, try another
The one, next to the other
That contains my joy
For me, oh boy!

No, not *that* one
Now you're just making fun
That is not nice
Don't make me ask twice

No, *not* the red
That one I dread!
That holds the brush
Come on now, rush!

My belly is not full
Not halfway at all
Yes, that's the one!
Woohoo, here comes my fun!

I'll sit by your feet
There's nothing so sweet
Then my oncoming treat
My day is complete!!

The Catch

I came into the house
Having caught a mouse
I was so proud
Your response was loud
I had a surprise for you!

You wondered what I had
And looked just a tad
Surprised at me
When you did see
What I'd brought in for you!

I caught it just for you!
What else could I do?
But bring it in
So my praise you'd sing
And, I spat it out, unchewed!

My work here is done
My, that was a lot of fun!
Let's get to bed
There's no more to dread
Until I catch another one!

The Cone of Shame

The 'cone of shame'
As it turns out
Is a very apt name
For it brings shame on me

It restricts my moves
I'm not sure what
You're trying to prove
Please take it off me!

I have no doubt
You think it worth
All of this clout
But I do not agree!

Tis but a scratch
No, not even
As much as that!
A teeny mark, you see?

So, take off this hood
Of course, I promise
I will be good
And not itch it merrily!

Well, maybe a little
Nothing much
Just a bit of a tickle
It is annoying me!

No, not again!
There is no need
To put that on, my friend
You are stifling me!

Hmm, so this is my lot?
That's just great
I'll definitely get mocked
When I go out to pee!

I am

I am your furbaby
Others you should tell
So, they know of your love
And value me as well

There is no one else
Who can care like me!
Or make you get off your butt
And exercise regularly!

With unconditional affection
We will spend our days
Just remember the unconditional bit
With my naughty ways!

None are really naughty
It is just how you perceive
The merit in an act of kindness
I may have bestowed on thee!

Did you say you're pregnant?

Did you say you're pregnant?
Well that is news to me
It will take some adjusting
But we can make room for he

I heard that you are pregnant
Well this is exciting news
I get to be big brother
And help (un)tie his shoes

It's ok I know he is human
So not as cute as me
It'll take a while for him to run
Or even walk properly

He'll have so much less hair to start
Quite bald in fact you see
But that will all come in time
And hairless is fine by me

He'll make some funny noises
So much louder than my standard chat
And probably make some choice smells
But I'm also well practiced at that

I know just where the best seat is
When he has his lunch
Haha, if you thought I was messy
Now here comes the crunch!

I'll do my best to catch it all
Together as a team
No droplet will go unmissed
We'll be cleaning in our dreams!

We'll enjoy sunny walks in the country
Or football in the park
I can't say I won't steal the ball
But I'll have good intentions at the start!

So, bring on the next stage
Step by step we stand tall
Welcome the new family member
Together we can face it all

I am a Little Terrier

I am a little terrier
I have no time to stop and stare
Unless of course you have some food
Then I am always there

No pigeon high or rabbit low
None can get past me
I am ever on the look out
For something in that darn tree

I'm watching for the bird up high
How those annoying little birds will sing
Sweet songs to tease and taunt me
Their necks I could just ring!

Seagulls, perhaps the worst of all
Intelligence flying way above
Oh, I wish I could grab one
I'd wear him like a glove!

The rabbit in the hedgerow
The hare crouching on its knees
I'm pretty sure I saw a squirrel
Running through the trees

Everyone, I know them
All shall bow, you'll see
For I am a Terrier!
The ruler of all? - Ah, that would be me!

Do not fear, I hear them all
Those pesky little rats
I'll take them down
And save us all
AND THAT MY DEAR IS THAT!

3. TERRIER OPINIONS

Ode to a Pigeon

Do not try to pass us
You cannot go unheard
We detect your every flutter
Your presence is observed

You live up in the branches
We see you in our trees
We did not invite you
Will you please just leave?

Or drop into the garden
Where we lie in wait
Ever ready for your presence
Come and meet your fate!

We are a pack of terriers
Can you hear us roar?
If Mum would only get the broom
We'll have pigeon in our store!

Stages of a Homecoming

1 . Wag your tail
This never fails

2. Give a shout
So, they're in no doubt

3. Bring a toy
That seems to bring all joy

4. Show a smile
There can be no denial

5. Give a kiss
An opportunity should not be missed

6. Check their bags
The smell of goodies will make you glad

7. Get outside too pee
Too much joy can trouble control, you see

8. Then return
A belly rub you've earnt

9. Have a drink at all cost
To replenish what you lost

10. Sit for your lead
Get ready for walkies to proceed!

Upside down

I like to lay on my back
Legs stretched in whatever direction
As long as they're slack
For when I'm upside down
At all my bits
You might frown
But I am much cooler
So, I cannot bother about that!
I will continue to be
An exhibitionist, yes indeed
So, if you don't like what you see
Then don't look at me!
I can't help it if you're shy?!
Be you woman or guy
So please don't dismiss
Or think me remiss
Just understand
For me, this *is* bliss!

The Mailman

I watch out for the mailman
The mailman bothers me
He says he just brings parcels
But I'm not so sure you see

I watch out for the mailman
His visits are a test
Though not it seems on Sundays
That's when I get my rest

He brings so many packages
Some look suspect, you'll see
I'm pretty sure they're dangerous
Though some could be for me

I watch out for the mailman
The mailman bothers me
I'll protect us all from the mailman
In case he isn't all he claims to be

The Chase

The thrill of the chase
Should not be misunderstood
For if you have ever been there
You'll know it feels good

Ok, may be not
If you are the object of the glee
But then I was talking about
How it feels for me!

New Ball

Ah ha! A new ball!
Lays amongst the pack
Its joys yet undiscovered
Its squeaker still intact!
This I must remedy
A true welcome give
Play its sweet melody
And show it the life it will live!

Difference of Opinion

Toodling

Today is for toodling
That's walking at slow speed
So don't expect me to run
Or bother to shout 'tout de suite'

I am busy toodling
Pottering is the best way
So you can call all you like
All the bloomin' day

I am just exploring
At a gentle pace
Join me why don't you?
There is no need to race!

Time

Why waste time?
Toodling is just fine
But I have things to see!

So off I trot
No, run, I'm off!
There is no way, you will catch me!

I cannot help
If you do yelp
At the thought of my speed

But life won't pass me by
I haven't the time
To toodle, idly!

No Whispers

I have to shout
For whispers
Have no clout
And all need
To hear me!
I have much
To say
Throughout
The day
So listen out
For me!
My words
Are those
Of wisdom
Stories I can tell
And of course
Great warnings
To others
I must yell!

Disagree

I do not agree
There is no need to shout
Sometimes a gentle whisper
Is sufficient, do not be a lout!
A soft communication
Is enough to convey
A simple message
And what you want to say
So there really is
No need to shout
Or be
Such a big lout!

First Trip To The Sea

I shimmer and shake
But will not break
I'm tougher than you see
I'll be fine, in no time
But you crossed the line
By putting me in the sea!
I was not prepared for the sensation
It really was a shock!
That water, well, it was moving!
Ha, you might laugh and mock!
But just remember what goes around
Comes around, you'll see!
A little bit like this body of water
So be prepared for retribution
Oh, yes indeed!
Now back to the present
You're right, I like it here
The water is soothing
And I like the sea air
The sand is also pleasing
I can dig about
So, I might forgive you
For this little journey out!

Come Get Me

Come join me, won't you?
Come join in my game
Look, I have found a ball
Without you it's not the same!

Come join me, won't you?
Let's bow to start our play
A sign of simple recognition
Of our oncoming fun conveys

Come catch me, won't you?
Or try, if you will!
We bop and weave, you can't catch me
Though you try, I won't keep still!

Ok, your turn!
That is only fair
Let's bow again, we are still friends
Come get me, I declare!

Call To Arms

I've found a mouse
Here!
Under the house!
Come see, come see, come see!

A call to arms
Friends!
Heed my alarm!
Come see, come see, come see!

Come on Dad
Lift!
Joys are to be had!
Come see, come see, come see!

Lift it true
Quick!
I'll save you!
You'll see, you'll see, you'll see!

That was fun
Yes!
Now I'm done!
Thank thee, thank thee, thank thee!

The Fly

I can hear you buzzing
All about my head
I wish you would buzz off
Or better, be dead

I am going to hunt you
Until you are gone
Then you'll realise
You buzzed for too long

I see you sitting
Perched above me
Don't think I can't catch you
It's all in the timing, you see?

Patience is a virtue
Persistence is key
Pouncing in perfect time
Will see you gone from me

I told you to buzz off
No, I've no regrets
I told you to buzz off
I was true to my threats!

Patrol

I take patrol seriously
My borders are divine
You may not cross them
For they are solely mine

I know if you've snuck in
And tried to steal from me
No, I am not having that
I patrol for the likes of thee

Patience

Whilst on patrol
I found your hole
Such a delight to me

I'll sit and wait
For you I hate
But also love to see

I could just dig
But then you'd twig
And risk setting you free

I will wait
I've set the bait
I am as patient as can be

Frog legs

I lay in a peculiar way
It helps me keep cool on a hot day
Though I also do it for fun
And the funny shape of my bum
It has a variety of names!
Frog legs, the splat or the sploot
No name for it is moot
Chicken spatchcock,
Pancake or whatever name you've got
I still think it is cute!

Zoomies

I can't think of a better way
To express my joy today
Than to tuck up my bum
Spring to start off the fun
And rush around like a loonie!

It is such fun, you see
To act the fool, yippee!
Join in the fun
Tuck up your bum
And try out your best zoomie!

4. LIFE ACCORDING
TO A TERRIER

The Reluctant Journey

I like a trip out in the car
Especially to the sea
But I also like woodland
Or to visit a friend or three

I am however not to be fooled
By your current pretence at glee
For I know only too well
When you're trying to pull one over me!

Yes, I sense the veterinary
In your new deceit
I am only too aware
As I sit faithfully by your feet

But I will reluctantly go
If indeed you insist
But I should warn you there's a
High chance of vomit, that can't be missed

Yes, the receptionist is very nice
I will not try to pretend
She is always so welcoming
A never distant friend

But I know exactly where I am
For this place smells of drugs and fear
And almost every dog I see
Also wants to be far from here

Most are actually just fine
And just in for a happy check
Some are just labradors
And they can be quite thick

Oh sorry, yes I know, that's not always true
And yes, they are all so sweet
But it doesn't change the undeniable fact
I've just vomited by your feet!

I warned you I was nervous
I didn't need to come!
I only came through the door
As you dragged me on my bum

Now here comes the veterinary
He has seen what's by your feet
You better tell him that's from motion sickness
Or the bill could be quite a feat!

Oh, I'm just in for a check!
Oh, what sweet relief!
I thought I was going to stay
I am glad it will be brief!

Hang on, what lie is this?
A needle, I do see!
I thought that blasted rustling
Was in fact a big fat treat!

Ouch, that stings, I've had enough
I suggest you take me home!
I'm really not quite sure when I'll forgive
I suppose I should have known?

You pull this trick every year
Declaring "all is well!"
Well, I suggest you inject yourself
And see how much you swell!

Too much you say? It's for my good?
Oh, so may it be!
But I suggest, you next time
Actually, take me to the sea!!

The Knock

Who are you?
Did I invite you to come?
What is your business here?
Are you prepared to scritch my bum?
If I really like you
You may get to see
My pink belly
And give it a rub for free!

If, however
I think you're foe, not friend
Then I suggest you leave
My loathing will not end
This is my warning
You've heard it fair
I will take you down
I ain't no Teddy bear!

Morning Rescue

Morning has broken
Please hurry up!
For there's tragedy unspoken
It's just my luck!
Look out the window
Oh, this just can't be!
I must go and educate
Will you just look in the tree?!
There is but a squirrel
The horror I cannot tell
That will befall us
If I don't go yell!
That tree rat is running
Amuck around me
And I'm pretty sure its stealing
Goodies from thee!
Oh, would you believe it?
Now there's a cat!
I absolutely am disgusted
I cannot have that!
No one can be trusted
No one, but me
Open the backdoor
I'll rescue you thee!!

I Can Hardly Tell

Of my current distress
I can hardly tell
I can't believe what happened
Though I saw it well
I chased that fat pigeon
Straight from the tree
Into the living room
It was meant for my tea
It flew true into the house
It was in my grasp
As it stunned itself
Upon the glass
And sad to say
I felt no shame
At the prospect of his end of days
Only glee was in my eyes
I had finally got that pigeon
Here came his demise!
And he was meant just for me
But alas, no!
Catastrophe!
For She heard the flutter too
And grabbed my prize
I wish it wasn't true
As to my huge surprise
She had some speed
Though rarely seen
It came in time to ruin me
And now that I am quite undone
I know she has foiled forever my fun
She caught my pigeon
And what happened next
I can barely say
For it can only vex
For the sorrow and shame

Will stay with me
Forever more, yes indeed
She took my pigeon
Straight outside
Photographed him?
And said goodbye!
Did she kill him?
Ring his neck?
Absolutely not
What the heck!?
She let him fly!
I wish it were
A slip of the hand
But in a blur
That she really did just understand
But sadly not
It would seem
And now that pigeon is back
To torture me
And what is worse
He brought his friend
Will this nightmare
Never end?!

My Ball

Ah, I think you must be new
So, I have a few quick words for you
You seem to have just found my ball
But you see, that's not one for all
That is indeed just for me
So, if you please, just leave it be
As you'll find of it, I'm rather fond
And we have an unbreakable bond
So just because you found it free
It really does just belong to me
Yes, I had quietly laid down
For a moment but, it's still my crown
It really does not quite suggest
I'd put it down for more than rest
So please return it now post haste
I'm in no mood to give you chase
I will however eternally be
Quite grateful if you return it easily
For if not, I fear you'll find
In me, a foe of fearful kind
Of the like, I doubt you'll ever see
Any worse, than the worst that there is in me
So please remove my ball from your mouth
And maybe return into the house
And there I'll leave it without so much as a sniff
And here we can leave off our tiff
But if you do really insist
A swift lesson from me will surely assist
In educating you of my sure ways
And lift you from your ignorant gaze
For that indeed IS my ball
It was NOT left out for one and all

Play

We had a squabble
Not a fight
In terrier world
That's a different plight!

Fear not
We are still friends
We know where
The line ends

Occasionally
We may cross
But rarely do
We stay at a loss

Rough and tumble
Is our way
Join us, won't you?
It's time to play!

Squeaker

The Squeaker!
Oh, to describe!
The joy I feel
Deep inside
Every time
I hear it call
It sings to me
It sings to all
It pleads for me
It to shake
To give a squeeze
It's squeak
To take
I really just
Can't help myself
When I hear
That squeaker Yelp!

New Addition

Of this new addition
I am very pleased!
It was so very exciting
When the news reacheth me!

I see it in its new home
Sitting round and fair
I hope it doesn't think me rude
Because I sit and stare?

Captive pure excitement!
That's all that I can see!
Waiting for the door to open
So, I can collect my tea!

I see no other reason
Why you would bring me that
Tasty looking rabbit
Who's sitting in that trap?

Pardon me? It is a pet?!!
Oh, no, not another one!?
Oh fine, I will just watch him!
Another, day I will have my fun!

My Bone

I will not moan
If I have my bone
I'll chew it happily

It tastes divine
And it is all mine
I do not share with thee

Get your own
I will not loan
This one easily

So off you trot
I care not a dot
If you're put out with me!

Broken

What is this? I cannot be sure
I fear some calamity
It looks just like my sacred rule
Totally broken, can it be?
What is *that*?
I can barely look, for fear of what I see
My peace has been shattered
A dark cloud has covered me

What is that on the chair?
Surely my eyes are deceiving me
I've spent my life protecting us
From villains such as he!
And now here you sit
Looking so darn pleased
Trying to it introduce
But you do not understand, you have ruined me!

Forever now my friends will disown
They'll have no time for me!
My favourite spot in the park I will forgo
For fear of mockery
Ah, yes for at me they will howl
And point and laugh and jeer
Eternally the bunt of all their jokes
For all my coming years

I've spent my life laughing
At the other folk
Whose guardians have been misguided
But now you've made me join their boat!
Oh, how will I bare it?
Oh, what misery has befallen me?
To smash my peace with no warning
And dashed my hopes for free!

You say I'm overreacting
We just need time to adjust
I'll realise that he is ok
And be friends, we must?
I say you are dreaming!
This will never be
With *that* a word will never be spoken
For all eternity!

Oh, good grief, can it get worse?
Now it's coming to me
It hasn't heard the rules yet
You run, I chase, you *flee*!
He says he wants to be friends?
At least to cohabit in peace
Well, you are deluded
Our war will never cease!

Have you not heard of Tom and Jerry?
The age-old story of cat and mouse?
Well, our story is just as well known
You cat, I dog – we don't live in one house!
Oh, the misery! The end, to which
I really cannot tell
What will become of me?
How will all things be well?!

Now, please keep this last bit
To your little self
For the only way I kept my street cred
Was to tell of lasting torture for myself
Well, in fact, that cat ain't half bad
Sometimes he is rather sweet
Somehow, we made a truce work
But remember, don't tell my friends on the street!

Chickens

I never see why you have chickens
They don't make sense to me
You say that they have purpose
But where? I cannot see
I'm not allowed to chase them
From me they have a free pass
And yet I see no other benefit
Of their feathered arse!
But you insist on keeping them
And so, they walk about the joint
I really think I am missing
The all-important point!

So You Bought a Puppy

So, you bought a puppy
What have you done to me?
You tell me to be grateful
It is a friend, I'll see?
I tell you you're mistaken
The horrors I can't tell
No, I don't believe
All *will* be well
Have you actually seen it?
It hardly stops to breathe
I wish it would just lie down
And not keep pestering me!
It hangs off my tail
And steals all my toys
Oh, this is ridiculous
I've never been more annoyed!
Why did you do it?
Life was good for me!
And now I'll never get peace
And I wish that I was free
You say that he will grow up?
When exactly will that be?
I'm pretty sure he has duracell
Tucked into his little seams
Haha, yes! he nipped you!
Now, will you learn?
See that puddle underneath the table?
That is not, of no concern
Oh, but he is oh, so cute?
That doesn't wash with me
I've seen what he is thinking
It is all quite obscene!

Oh ok, he has some ways
That are rather dear
He seems to be sharing
The ideals I revere
Maybe I can teach him?
And we can share a toy?
I must admit that sharing
Does seem to bring us joy
Oh fine, I admit it!
You might be right indeed
I think in him I've found a friend
A partner in crime?.. we'll see.

The Journeyman

I had a great adventure
Whilst on my walk
So many lovely places
And dogs with which to talk

I went up on the hills
And there I met a Collie
I was surprised to learn
His joy for work is not folly

He is really enthusiastic
About his job every day
And actually, enjoys doing
Exactly what his master says

He herds sheep with style
Speed and such skill
I really was impressed
But I left him up the hill

For my place is not herding
In that skilful, deliberate way
I'd prefer to scatter them
And in the fields play

So, I ventured downwards
Down into the woods
And again, was surprised
Who was in the neighbourhood!

There I met a Spaniel
His tail wagging fast
I had heard a gunshot
And he came running past

He grabbed a fallen pheasant
With impressive accuracy
But I was more surprised
At what he then told me

I thought he had caught dinner
I congratulated on the size
But he did tell me
It was not his prize!

He collected for his master
Retrieved with delicacy
And oh, so gently
Laid it by his master's knee!

Now this is all well and all
But it's not for me
I prefer a partnership
Where my spirit can follow free!

I continued on my ramble
On paths to and fro
I saw some beautiful places
Some places we both know

I checked out lots of hedgerows
The odd ditch, didn't worry me
I checked out a few rabbit holes
I chased a squirrel up a tree!

I very much enjoyed my time out
I liked the scenery
But I would have preferred it
If you had also come with me

You shouldn't have left the gate open
I couldn't resist the opportunity
To stalk that blasted fox
Who keeps stinking up our tree!

By the way I found him!
Or rather his big hole
I barked and dug for a while
But in the end, decided to go

I'm pretty sure he got the hint
That he is not welcome near me
I left a little present
Next to his big tree!

Finally, on my way home
I passed by the blue house
The one at the end of the street
With the dog the size of a mouse

He yaps like a kitten!
It's such a shame to see
A dog about as threatening
As a newborn puppy!

Though apparently his humans
Have a sense of humour too
As they also have a St Bernard
His name is Big Baloo

He really is enormous
The biggest bear you'll see!
I hope he doesn't sit on the other
As it'll be the end of him, definitely!

He is a decent guard dog
I will give him that
But not so impressive
As he also lets in the cat!

Anyway, I'm home now
Many adventures I could tell
We're both glad I'm home
So, there is no need to yell

I promise I will wait for you
Next time I need to go out
I know the best places
You'll love all that's about!

5. FAMILY

Mother

Oh, my word I'm pregnant!
I'm not sure that I understood
Quite all of the consequences
Of my liaison in the neighbourhood

Ah, but I'm excited!
I'm in the mothering mood
I'll be ever so doting
When I meet my little brood

I'm feeling rather heavy
My belly is oh, so round
I've never ever known it
To hang so near to the ground!

I feel the puppies wiggling
Even you can see
How they are all squirming
So much within my round belly!

Good grief! I'm glad that's over
No one did ever tell
How very exhausting is labour
But now all is well!

I have my sweet babies
They are all surrounding me
I know them all by number
Count one and two and three

I'm not sure what to call them?
I'll leave that up you
I'll concentrate on feeding them
And cleaning up their poo

I look at them while sleeping
Full of pride I sit and stare
An ever-loving Mother
No better ever was there

Ah, now they're walking
Good grief, do they stop?
I think it's time you bring in
Their father from round the block!

Now they are all spoken for
By forever loving homes
My everlasting joy unspoken
As my babies are rehomed

I never will forget them
But my job is well done
My love will last unbroken
I know my rest I've won

My babes have now all flown the nest
Exciting times untold
To share the love, they received
New adventures to unfold

Father

I am your Father
It's an easy life for me
I take a lot of credit
But your Mum does it all, you see

I'll largely leave you
To your Mother's care
There's not much I can do anyway
Your Mother doesn't like to share

When you're a little bigger
Some interest I will make
Especially if you have food
Or a toy I want to take

But what is a Father realistically
Really, going to do?
Other than occasionally pop-in
To check on all of you?

And inspect to see if you resemble
Me in any small way
If are as handsome
Perhaps you can stay

Yes, I'll enjoy the odd game
A ball game we could play
But when I am tired
With your Mother you can stay

Then at all your viewings
In you I'll take my pride
But really, I want those visitors
To 'ooh' over me, with attentive sighs

You, may be somewhat cuter
But I can jump easily
Right up on the sofa
And claim their laps for me!

Ah! to be a Father
It's the life, you'll see!
Loving all the ladies
And keeping all the credit for me!

Parent And Child

I heard you the first time
I am not so deaf
Though I might be in a minute
If your decibels do not cleft
You are too outspoken
For this time of the day
I'll be there in a moment
Why don't you go and play?
There's toys all around you
Some are barely touched
The squeaker in the squirrel
Is a little much
Go for one of the quiet ones
A rope or a ball
Maybe a crinkly one
That's not the worst of all
Just give me a minute
To wake up, ok?
There's only so much excitement
I can take at this time of day!

Renewed Life

Oh, for goodness sake
Not again!
When will you learn?
You drive me round the bend
I am trying to sleep
I suggest you do too
And when you're awake
Find something else to do!

I admire your energy
But we do not share
Your enthusiasm
For what may be there!
I've made my peace
With those about
They keep to themselves
And do not shout

The mouse and cat
Can fight it out
The chickens flap
Of that there is no doubt
But they live outside
So, that's fine by me
And I am free to sleep
Undisturbed you see

I give you leave
To go outside
Do what you will
To keep occupied
When you're old
You'll understand
What it's like
For this old man!

Hmm, maybe your joy
Might awaken in me
A spark of life I thought
Long gone, you see?
I suppose I could
Have a quick game
Will life ever be dull again?
Who'da thought, it would be
That you bring out, the puppy in me?

Father and Son

Now my Son, you are a Terrier
There is much for you to learn
Your Mother will teach you all that's fair
But I am here to help you discern

For there is much to understand
About how to get your way
And not just be a sheep
And do exactly what your people say

You have to train them
Make them see things your way
And even better if
They think it was their idea, ok?

It will take many an hour
But fear not, my boy
Before you know it
They'll be showering you with toys

First thing to learn is 'puppy eyes'
You inherited those from me
All you have to do is look at them
And they will melt, you'll see!

Make sure to do this quickly
If you detect angry tones
For resistance is futile then
And they won't continue with their moans

They'll tell shoes are not for eating
Nor cables or the TV remote
But they will learn if they leave it out
This rule was put to your vote

I do not advise cables
They are actually bad, you see
But anything else is yours to test
Or them to clear away quickly!

When they are eating
Be sure to stay near
Gently gazing, patiently waiting
Food will be yours, have no fear!

If they have children
Be sure to seek them first
They are the soft touch
And drop things the worst

This is a win-win situation
As you're helping to clean up
A very useful service
No one is gonna call you, a mucky pup!

Now, should someone trip on you
Or risk some injury
Be sure to call out in distress
Then their guilt must be remedied

Normally with a treat
But a hug, cuddle, kiss or game
Are all quite acceptable
Means of dispensing with their shame

Some people can be a little slow
At realising quite how fun balls are
So, if yours doesn't get the hint
Repeatedly rolling yours will get you far

Roll it at their feet
As many times as you can
Failing that, give a little woof!
And they'll get with the plan!

Always wag your tail!
Express yourself with glee
Let them know when they've been good
And show you are also happy

You will quickly learn the treat packet
A sound that will always thrill
Pay attention to the location
And point there as often as you will!

Some you may have to earn
With the odd little trick
But mostly that is ok
As you'll enjoy dancing like a lunatic!

You will guard your people
Against foes unknown
But you do it valiantly
And maintain your terrier throne

All kinds of critters may trial you
But you should be prepared for all
Be it spider, rat or pigeon
Rabbit, cat or even squirrel

Larger dogs should be no issue
For though they may win by weight
They are no match for your wit
So, who rules, is not up for debate!

They can usually be befriended
And are useful play buddies
Or are at least target practice
For taking things down to their knees!

The hairy ones are the most useful
Especially on cold days
They make excellent pillows
I doubt you'll need a duvet!

You will quickly work out who is family
And who in fact is foe
Most are actually visiting to worship you
This is how life should be so

The people that are worthy
Will cherish all you do and say
Take you to exciting places
And cuddle you at the end of the day

They will laugh at all your jokes
And appreciate your unique charm
Realise you are selectively deaf
When there is danger to disarm

Do not explore too far
For to home, you must always return
But by all means test the boundaries
Otherwise how *is* your human to learn?!

Guard your family valiantly
Love them for all your days
Have fun and explore your world
Be true to your Terrier ways!

6. INTRODUCING...

Norfolk Terrier

I am a Norfolk Terrier
What exactly does that mean?
I tend to be a little chubby
Or am so-called by those who are obscene

I actually think it is just padding
No, not even that
I'm not responsible for genetics
And that's a fact!

Ok, I'm a little boxy
A compact hunting machine
I was bred to go through straw barns, hedges
Maybe even the odd stream

I can do agility
But I'm not really built for speed
Though you can build up my stamina
And impress others of my breed

I am not a simple dog
Though occasionally it would seem
I have given my Mum cause to question
If this statement is quite supreme

I do have a tendency
To cause the odd spat
I didn't really think it through
And perhaps that's why earlier, I was called a prat?

It could be possible
I thought it fun
To maybe, yes, maybe
Just nip someone up the bum

They were then passing me
It was just for a little fun
But I did not contemplate
The owner of said bum

For it was a different terrier
One whom as it seems
Is slightly more feisty
If he is ruffled by the likes of me

Now, sense would say to walk away
And apologise as I retreat
But I am a terrier
And cannot admit defeat!

Praise be! Here's Mum
She'll save the day, she will defend me!
Hurrah! I win, that was fun
I think I've earnt my tea!

Now, I've had my exercise
And worked up quite a sweat
Praise the Lord, I do have some food
Waiting for me yet!

I am a compact terrier
Oh, don't be so mean!
I heard you fill in with 'chubby'
Fine, say whatever, it won't bother me!

My Mum, she loves me exactly as I am
And knows how things should be
For I am an affectionate lad
An absolute devotee

I am a friendly terrier
And actually, get on with all I meet
People big or small, I like them all
And they love me as I sit cutely by their feet

Despite my little confession
I like other dogs as well
But when I am excited, I just can't completely switch off
My cheeky, charming spell!

There is just one more task ahead
Before I end my day
One prized destination waits for me
Yes, on the sofa, I must lay!

Cairn Terriers

How to describe a Cairn terrier?
Hmm, where to start?
To tell of their huge character
Or the size of their heart?

Their heart is undeniable
So loyal and so true
But also, very independent
Their minds they know, not you

'Spirited' just about covers it
Feisty, busy little bees
Checking out all places
Critters might have been

Mischief they might get in
But with no malice by intent
They were just investigating
This makes their heart content

A sense of humour is essential!
But if in them you put your trust
You never will regret it
Having a Cairn terrier is a must!

Presence

The way I move is rather neat
I trot along as I lift my feet
You will know me by my swagger
Oh, so light, I do not stagger
I lift my tail with such pride
I have presence when I stride
Every head to me shall turn
A Cairn is passing, watch and learn!

Jack Russell and Hunt Terriers

The Jack Russell comes in various forms
It should be white with tan or black
They can be smooth or scruffy
But either makes a beautiful Jack!

Independent, yet affectionate
Charming in everyway
Intelligent and so cheeky
They'll warm your heart every day

Fun for all the family
Loyal and ever true
Ready for adventures
They'll always be there for you

Then there is the Hunt Terrier
They also get called Jack
But are really quite different
Though the origin of the Jack pack

Solid in colour
Chocolate or black with tan
Sleek and beautiful
They speed across the land

Energetic little people
Ready to be on the go
Always on the look out
For almost any scenario!

They really are affectionate
And love a cuddle every day
But need plenty of exercise
A chance to run, hunt and play

The Airedale

I am the King of Terriers
I rule the pack you see
Of them I am the largest
And fiercest I definitely be

It is my job to guard them
None shall ever pass unheard
I see and hear you whether
You be man or beast or bird

My call to arms will never go unanswered
Alert little pack are we
We are ever there and waiting
Please do not underestimate me!

I am the King of Terriers
I am in charge of all
Ok, I answer to my Mother
But she understands my call!

I am the King of Terriers
Please make no mistake
From my deep slumber
I will be quick to awake

I am the King of Terriers
No more handsome will you see
I hope you have a sense of humour
As I tell my jokes for free

I am the King of Terriers
None shall pass by me
I am the most loveable
The King of all I see

Pebbles

My name is Pebbles
Short and sweet like me
Though it does have a variation
Or maybe even three

The first is Pebble-lina
An affectionate extra name
For I am cute and lovely
So, I take this with no shame

Then there is Rebel- Pebble
I'm not sure that suits me
As I am no rebel
Like I said, I'm sweet, you see?

Lastly, well it is offensive
But I will agree
Maybe I have earnt this
Though Mum is not funny

They call me Boulder!
How rude can they be?
Yes, I include Dad in this
I think he was the instigator, you see

I do like my food a lot
So, at times I am rounder than I should be
But I suggest Mum looks at her own waistline
Before she comes mocking me!

I enjoy a hearty toodle
A turnabout outside
I may even hunt things
But this doesn't fill my time

I am a lady of leisure
Exuberance is not for me
Though I do like to call out
And watch the others dance about with glee

What do I do the rest of the time?
If play is only relative to me?
And pottering is well and all
But doesn't long prove key?

I will tell you what I do!
For I do it well
My days are spent propping up cushions
On the sofa I do dwell!

I lay about and watch TV
All kinds of programmes amuse me
Dogs and cats, I might like best
But I am not too fussy, you see

Lastly, I will tell you
Of my little party trick
Just in case someone dares
Accuse me of being thick!

Attention is guaranteed
No one can deny
When I wave my paw
And give a sweet, high five!

So, regardless of name, I am the One
That you'll find on the sofa, making my own fun
Waiting for cuddles, a little TV
With a smile, none better, will you see!

Queenie

I am the ruler of a dynasty
There is no other like me
I am the founder of a passion
An appreciation society

I have a name, it is very fitting
You should know it oh, so well
For I founded my own nation
And on this my thoughts do often dwell

I need you to pay homage
To humbly bend the knee
At the point of my arrival
Or room occupancy

My daughter is Milady
A name that is only right
For one that will succeed me
One dark and fatal night

But in the cold truth of it
There is only One, that's me!
A powerful ruler
No less than Royalty!

I rule the roost, unquestioned
By no man, beast or bird
Nothing flies above or below unnoticed
No, nothing is unheard

I have been called a Diva
What to ignorance can I say?
I just give them a smile
And carry on with my day!

Grooming Queenie

I hear you think I need grooming
We really don't agree
Who decides what's tidy
Or actually scruffy?
I'm not sure to whom you've spoken
I really cannot tell
My dear you should have spoken
To one who knows very well

As I am just perfect
Exactly as you see
For nature has designed me
To be hairy and it flow free
To express myself in all my hairy glory
So the sun doesn't bother me
Nor wind or rain, that is no pain
While my hair so covers me.

I realise it may get too long
Or knots may start to be
Well, my dear then just brush it
Though don't fuss over me
But rather make a swift job
And you will surely see
A little was just enough
To keep me as handsome as I should be!

Milady

My mother is Queenie
Everyone knows her name
For she is quite cheeky
But I can be the same
The apple really didn't fall
Far from the tree
So please believe
I am also Royalty

I am just more subtle
Than my Mum can be
She's a bit of a diva
I'll tell you that for free
Just don't tell her I said so
As she might be mad
But I am just as keen at hunting
Definitely better than my Dad

I also take after my Father
Of that there is doubt
I look rather like him
And share his love to shout
Not in a bad way
A cute call, you'll see
Just so I can say hello
And earn a chin scratch or three!

Ollie

As our meeting begins
I will present my chin
So be prepared
To scratch me there
If my approval
You want to win!

If you are truly graced, I'll say
'Hello' in my own special way
For I am rather apt
At vocalising that
So, standby
To be blown away!

Gentleman Duke

I am The Duke
I'm very bright
But more than that
I am a gorgeous sight

For that is a fact
So, much tis true
For all see me,
Look twice and not at you

I am The Duke
An affectionate lad
The hugs I give
Are the best you'll have had

I am The Duke
What else can I say?
If I have my ball
Then all is Ok

My favourite is spiky and blue
That is absolutely the one, it's true
There are many others but of them all
It's that one that I call MY ball

Frustration comes when a friend
Implores of me my ball to lend
I say implore, but I mean steal
For it is not by choice, its merits I reveal

But I am, however, a sporting chap
And share I will and that is that
I am truly a gentle friend
And for a good game, I will lend

As long as we play fair, you see
And they don't in fact just steal from me
That behaviour is not nice
And lend again? No, I won't play twice

I will just turn around and run
And make my own playful fun
So, just please remember me
I am The Duke, true gentleman of all you'll see!

Ninja

My name is Ninja
Not the most feminine of names
But once you've met me
You'll see it fits all the same

Not only am I dark and sleek
No one zooms like me
Athletic in my physique
As beautiful as can be

I doubt there's many faster
Then when I'm at top speed
The height at which I can jump
Will impress all who witness me

I am an affectionate Ninja
I love a belly rub
I will throw my self-right at you
So, be prepared for my love!

Xena

When I was a baby
I was a lucky pup
I was born into a happy home
The ideal way to grow up

My Mother lived so happy
Loved and cared was she
Surrounded by her friends
And members of the family

I had five brothers
That was just fine by me
For though I was the only sister
I was feisty enough, you see

When they named me
They worked me out well
Not only was it amusing
It had a good ring, like a bell

My name is Xena!
Xena The Warrior Princess
Like I said, befitting
For one made for success!

Percy

P is for Percy
Of that there's no doubt
And if you should call him
You won't need to shout

For he is only too happy
To be right beside you
An affectionate chap
This is very true

But should you call out
For another name
That ends in Y or IE
You'll find he has no shame

For to you he will answer
With just as much glee
Looking up expectant
For treats to be free

See, you actually meant Percy
Not the lesser name
So, he came a trotting
And he saved you any pain

A smile so infectious
It will remove any doubt
That you had meant a different dog
When originally, you did shout!

Wilson

You can only call me
If you are willing to exclaim
In joyful expression
As though you are insane!

You can pronounce it
Sounding rather drab
But I will renounce you
Until your call is absolutely fab!

Spread your arms open wide
Preferably bend the knee
Enunciate with pride
As you call for me!

I will come a-running
Running at such speed
I may forget my brakes
So, prepare to catch me!

There is a good chance
I also brought a ball
So, please prepare yourself
For a game to play and all!

Stanley

They often call me Stanley
Though it is actually just Stan
'Stan the Man' is my title
If you've met me, you'll understand
For I am the origin
Of all these terrier prose
And I am the one that keeps
Everybody on their toes!

I am now rather ancient
My best days have been run
But that will never mean
My glory is undone!
For I am the very beginning
Of all that came to be
A terrier passion and leader
Of all that you see!

My rule has been passed down
To one more energetic than me
Though I'm still outspoken
And give my words out for free
For there is much wisdom
To be had from this old man
So, don't forget I've chosen
On you my knowledge to expand

I'm charming, handsome and cheeky,
A friendly little chap
Adventures, some unspoken
I'll never forget any of that
I'll always be the founder
Of this crazy lot
Another quite as me, can
Absolutely not be got!

So, as I now sit back
And enjoy my well earnt rest
I will watch over everyone
As there is no test
To quite how wonderful
Life with me has been
So many adventures we have had
So many places we have seen

I was a faithful co-pilot
I knew how to drive your truck
And take us to those places
Where you made your buck
Then we'd go on days out
When you were free
All before our retirement
And old age got the better of me

I do not regret it!
No, not at all
I had fun every minute
Especially when acting the fool
Everyone, I charmed them!
They would all agree
To meet little Stanley
Is something special, yes indeed!

7. CONCLUSIONS

Life with a Terrier

I am a little terrier
My size doesn't bother me
I have plenty of character
Its oozing out of me

I may be small and cutesy
But don't be fooled by me
You've never seen such character
In one twice the size, you'll see

Other dogs may tower above
That doesn't frighten me
My dear, I am a terrier
And all shall bend the knee

Yes, they may well all be cute
And wag their tails happily
But none are quite as intelligent
Or have half the personality

Ok, they may be more obedient
And return when called with glee
But I might call that ignorance!
And they should learn to follow me

Yes, I heard you the first time!
But this hole looks quite new
And I'm pretty sure that as a terrier
I'm expected to run free and true

Ah ha, my dear, I'm on my way!
Oooh, but no, could it be?
Alas, that mole hill is quite fresh
I must explore indeed

Oops, yes, my name again you shout
I know you won't leave me
I'm on my way, there is no doubt
I'm in trouble to some degree

My work isn't always appreciated
But my heart is always true
I'm always out to defend and slay
Those who are not for you!

You wanted a dog with character
Well that's just fine by me
I am more than spirited
And I'll throw cheek in for free!

Yes, I am a terrier
I don't care how much I cost
I like to roll in the mud
And stay out with the frost

Well, I am a terrier
It's a feisty life for me
I may cause the occasional groan
But I'll always be home for tea!

I am a terrier!
You can't stay mad at me!
Just look into my eyes!
And tell me the best things in life aren't free?!

Oh yes, I am a terrier!
Just look upon my face
I will wipe away each said
Misdemeanour and apparent disgrace

Haha, indeed I made you laugh
How could you be angry at me?
For yes, I am a terrier
And trouble just follows, see?

Ok, so why have a terrier?
They just sound like a pain
Of course, I am! But that's alright
You'll love me all the same!

Ah ha, I am a terrier!
And there is no one else like me
I am THE very best of them
If you've met one, you'll agree

You cannot possibly live without
A terrierist, you'll see
For fun and laughter follow
A charming chap like me

In advance I will say sorry
For the trouble I may cause
But in truth you asked for it
So, the trouble must be yours

I'll always be beside you
In good times and bad
Forever part of the family
Such fun the like you'll have never had

All of this I guarantee
Life together will be swell
We'll take each day, in our particular way
And together say, ALL IS WELL!

The Dog

The dog is no bicycle, car or TV
They are not property to be discarded,
As nothing, carefree
They are family, with four legs not two
But are undoubtedly family
You should realise this through and through
If you are looking for a fair-weather friend
Or can't appreciate this fact
Then please just suspend
Any notion of having a dog in your life
As you will miss all benefits
And the dog live with strife
A dog is not temporary
Is not for a time
A dog is forever
Forever by your side
Though I sing the praises of my terrier friends
All dogs are worthy
And to you, their love lend
No, not lend, for they do not retract
Once you are theirs
There's no looking back
Forever family
Forever loved
Forever walking by your side
No doubt of their affection
It does not ebb with the tide
Together you step through life's to's and fros
Together sharing
So much that no one else really knows
Knows of the treasure
That loving a dog gives
How much it opens up your heart
And let's you really live
Yes, one day, you will have to part

But until that dark day
Such joys will impart
Joys that, otherwise, you would have missed
Forever missing something
In that sloppy kiss!
They are your family
Together and a day
It doesn't end there
It sounds like it may
But it doesn't
For family always remains
Remains In spirit
And walks with you, across life's plains
For now, your heart is open
To canine love, all divine
A true love, unspoken
You should not deny
For in loving a second
You honour the first
Acknowledging the opening
Of your heart, that can't be reversed
You'll never replace!
That cannot be done
But you can fill a void
And continue to run
Life's winding path
In loving memory
Of your furbaby
Who set your heart free

Epilogue

Now if you have read through to here
And if you're still smiling
And thinking a terrier dear
Then you have probably passed the first test
Assuming your circumstances
Match us no less!
Then there's just but one thing to decide
With which breed of terrier is best to reside?
For there are many
And none are quite the same
And although often described as a collective here
There are many traits that each hold dear
Dear but different
With different creeds
So please properly research all of our needs!
The Airedale, the largest of terriers, there's no doubt
Is not for the faint of heart or easily pulled down
Loving and loyal
Enjoys comedy
But not everyone appreciates all about these!
Cairns are so spirited, intelligent and fair
But do not be fooled
You have met your match there!
They are quite capable of working you out
And if you don't keep them active
Then they'll want to move out!
Jack Russells are active, energetic little peas
That need to be mentally stimulated
And don't do well if bored so, please
Only bring one, into your home
If from your home, you are going to regularly roam!
Then there is the Norfolk
Who lazier can be!
But is still very much a terrier
So, very much needs

Proper exercise, love and to be trained
Otherwise it is you, that will be reigned!
There are many other beautiful terrier breeds
Please look into them all
And decide which meets your needs
From Westie, Border or the Scott
Lakeland, Welsh or even a Fox
All are wonderful little dogs
So, go forth and let the love knock you off your socks!

The Breeder

My story as a breeder?
Where exactly shall I start?
I suppose from the beginning
And at the beginning is my heart

For all my hairy charges
Each one I hold so dear
In fun and love and laughter
But also when we share our tears

On the whole, it is a privilege
Of the like I cannot tell
For all those who know me
Know only too well

I'm not very good expressing
Exactly what I want to say
But I'll do my best in poem form
My feelings to convey

The joys that surround me
All have a waggy tail and four legs
And active personalities
That in some, causes dread

But to me they are a blessing
A true joy of no small size
A privilege that continues
Every day to surprise

There can be no dull moment
With packs such as these
They are there through thick and thin
Ever happy for me to please

I know them all individually
I know their unique ways
Some I can't quite describe
But I know them through love and play

Some are big comedians
Some are oh, so soft
Some are troublemakers
Most just a mixture of the lot!

Yes, we have our ups and downs
Some really sadden me
But every day I carry on
And they love always for free

Their trust for granted, I do not take
A blessing I earn each day
Especially when they put their trust in me
To safely give their babes away

For we have all put all our love
Into every single pup
Our best to raise them every day
With everlasting love

So, if from us a puppy we do grant
Feel the privilege and the joy
But most of all, carry on our love
And keep him well supplied with toys!

For that is my purpose
The very point of me
To raise my dogs with love and care
I hope this is my legacy

The Author

My name is Alexia
What rhymes with that?
Nothing much useful
I'm pretty sure of that!
I have lived a quiet life
In the Suffolk country
Living in one village
My family didn't roam far, you see!
I live here with my husband
The patient Sergio
Together we love all creatures
But terriers caught our hearts so!
So, now with them we live and breathe
An excellent way to be
Incredibly lucky to live, in terrier company!
We have learnt to appreciate
Cheeky terrier ways
So, I thought I'd write some down
As our cheeky terriers would say!
I hope you find the humour
Love and passion there
For life with a terrier
Is extraordinarrier!

Photo credit: Sergio Muelle